Original title:
In the Walls of Memory

Copyright © 2025 Creative Arts Management OÜ
All rights reserved.

Author: Jude Lancaster
ISBN HARDBACK: 978-1-80587-192-7
ISBN PAPERBACK: 978-1-80587-662-5

The Secret Language of Echoes

Deep inside this silly mind,
A riddle laughs, a joke entwined.
Whispers bounce from wall to wall,
Mocking all who dare to call.

Curly memories twist and spin,
Like socks that vanish in the din.
They chuckle soft, then giggle bright,
As shadows dance in morning light.

Windows into Lost Tomorrows

Peeking out at future quests,
Where jokes and laughter take their rest.
Silly faces in the glass,
Winking at my dreams that pass.

Time's a jester, half awake,
With funny pies and silly cakes.
Sliding windows, snappy scenes,
Warping time like silly jeans.

A Gallery of Unspoken Words

Pictures hang, with smiles and frowns,
Whimsical hats and funny gowns.
Silent whispers fill the air,
While grinning ghosts play tag with flair.

Each canvas drips with quirk and cheer,
A giggle framed, a friendly sneer.
The art of laughter comes alive,
As chuckles gather, they all jive.

Time's Fragmented Tapestry

Threads of joy weave in and out,
Silly patterns leave no doubt.
Each stitch a giggle, bright and loud,
A patchwork quilt of laughter proud.

Misplaced buttons, knots and more,
Time trips lightly on the floor.
Tickles found in seams we mend,
Creating joy that's hard to end.

A Tapestry Stitched with Sacrifice

In corners where echoes blend,
Laughter dances, it won't end.
A tapestry of silly sights,
Weaving joy from foolish fights.

Each thread a tale of blunders bold,
Of secrets shared, and stories told.
Stitches made from giggles bright,
In fabric soft, we find our light.

Memories Stowed in Dust

In boxes piled high with fluff,
Lie tales of letting go of tough.
Dust bunnies store our brightest quips,
Of sneezes, trips, and milkshake sips.

Forgotten snacks beneath the bed,
Whiskered dreams that dance in our head.
Each little crumb a saga shared,
As laughter lingers, unprepared.

The Script of Echoing Silence

In spaces where whispers run amok,
The silence holds a quirky clock.
Tick-tock goes the giggling air,
Moments trapped without a care.

Scripts of silence, plays unseen,
Where nobody's right, and all are keen.
We mime our joy in awkward ways,
And fill the void with silly plays.

The Compass of Loss

A compass spins, points to the past,
Where laughter echoes, built to last.
We chart our course on maps of glee,
Through paths of jest, so wild and free.

In circles drawn with crayon dreams,
We steer through life's ridiculous schemes.
Finding treasure in each misstep,
With every blunder, we laugh, we prep.

The Library of Regrets

Forgotten tales in dusty scrolls,
My awful jokes take center roles.
Librarians sigh with knowing glances,
As I fumble through my life's romances.

Each shelf a wish I'd left untold,
A story of me, a sight so bold.
Stumbling over tales I've spun,
Laughing at how I thought I'd won.

Stories Stuck Between the Bricks

Whispers trapped, like socks in dryers,
Puns multiple, oh, how they tire!
Doodle notes in margins wide,
Bricks chuckle as I try to hide.

Old jokes echo, bouncing 'round,
Each memory lost, but laughter found.
Stuck between cracks, they play and tease,
Reminding me, nothing's meant to please.

A Journey Through Dusty Hallways

Dust bunnies leap like little goats,
Creepy tales hidden with silly notes.
I trip on memories, oh what a thrill,
Each corner I pass gives me a chill.

Timid ghosts giggle, float above,
They nudge me back when I speak of love.
A hall of laughter, a maze so bright,
Where forgetfulness takes flight at night.

Windows to the Past

Peeking through panes with smudged designs,
Stories whistle like old train lines.
Time winks at me, a cheeky sprite,
I laugh at snapshots in awkward light.

Memories dance like leaves on air,
Through open windows, we all share.
Faded frames tell jokes so cracked,
Each laugh a story, joyfully stacked.

Time's Accordion of Echoes

Once I saw a clock that danced,
Ticking tunes while I just pranced.
It twisted time, a show so bright,
Made minutes laugh and hours light.

Underneath a bed, a shoe was found,
It claimed it traveled all around.
With tales of mountains, rivers, stew,
I wonder what my left sock knew.

Old chairs tell jokes of creaks and squeaks,
Whispers shared through the sleepy weeks.
They giggle in the nightly shade,
Of all the mischief they once played.

Oh, time is such a playful sprite,
It stretches days and leaps at night.
In every bend, a memory stows,
With silly grins that time bestows.

Lighthouses in the Fog of Memory

There's a lighthouse with a quirky beam,
It lights the way for my lost dreams.
A seagull jokes, on a fence post, waits,
To share the tales of seabird fates.

In the fog, my grandmother's dish,
Made of memories and sweetened fish.
Each bite a laugh, a splash of glee,
She swore that none would ever flee.

A treasure chest of silly shoes,
Each pair holds secrets, none to snooze.
They plot a party with mismatched flair,
And dance around without a care.

In this fog, the laughter roams,
Where every shadow calls me home.
With all these lights, I can't go wrong,
For in the haze, I sing along.

The Cloister of Hidden Remains

In a room with socks that don't match,
Old photos find memories to hatch.
A cat that thinks it's a king,
Ruling over things that make us sing.

Crispy snacks from long-ago feasts,
Silly stories shared like beasts.
A duster that dreams of being gold,
When all it really does is fold.

Blankets stacked like ancient lore,
Each one hiding tales galore.
The clock that ticks a funny beat,
Tickling toes, oh, what a treat!

Voices echo, all in jest,
Within these walls, we're truly blessed.
Reflecting light of days gone by,
A laughter that will never die.

Time-Cast Shadows of Belonging

In corners where odd shoes reside,
Ghosts of laughter take a ride.
A pile of laundry, a sight to see,
Proclaims its reign over you and me.

The floorboards creak with stories told,
About the time we dared be bold.
A wig that once danced at a prom,
Now stashed away, oh what a bomb!

Chairs that squeak like they are wise,
Knowing secrets, letting out sighs.
The fridge hums tunes of days gone past,
Like a DJ, spinning tracks so fast.

With each shadow that flickers by,
Archiving laughter and the why.
In a cozy nook where all feels right,
Our memories twirl in pure delight.

The Chamber of Longing

Old toys whisper dreams of play,
From yesterday to today.
Dust bunnies waltz in the sun's glow,
Sharing secrets that they know.

A sofa springs with a creaky laugh,
Holding tales of a misguided path.
A window with a view so bright,
Asks, what happened to that kite?

Frames hold faces we barely recall,
With expressions that could make us fall.
The fridge claims leftovers of fame,
Though they all reek of old college names.

In this room of mixed memories,
The past is hinted in gentle keys.
Where longing dances, funny yet true,
And each glance tells something new.

Whispers in the Forgotten Hall

Footsteps echo in silence so loud,
While boots laugh, feeling quite proud.
Dust motes twirl like shy debutantes,
In shadows where a grumpy cat haunts.

Old coats hang like memories worn,
In this hall where legends are born.
A rug that curls up like a cat,
Hiding stories of a playful spat.

Toys that giggle at the dark,
Sharing secrets from a spark.
The scent of cake long gone stale,
Reminds us of a sweetened tale.

In whispers soft as a gentle breeze,
Time flickers like the rustling trees.
Laughter lingers, a cheerful call,
Finding joy in the forgotten hall.

Voices from Shadowed Corners

Whispers hang like laundry lines,
Breezes dance through forgotten signs.
Socks lost in time, a shoe in a tree,
Laughter echoes just out of spree.

A cat leaps high, it thinks it can fly,
Chasing old dreams that flutter and sigh.
Silly shadows play tag on the wall,
While dust bunnies dare not start a brawl.

Ghosts of Longing in Quiet Rooms

Old chairs creak with tales untold,
But the tea's gone cold, so bold.
Mismatched socks keep a secret stash,
While the lamp flickers in subtle cash.

A grandmother clock is late to the show,
Ticking and tocking with nowhere to go.
Cushions sigh as if they could speak,
Trading old stories, oh so unique!

Tapestries of Time Yet Unraveled

Laces untied on shoes of the past,
Running fast, but how long can it last?
Grandpa's stories, a yarn that won't end,
Socks under beds where dust bunnies blend.

Curtains that flutter, a soft little dance,
Remembering moments that missed their chance.
Knitting old patterns with laughter and glee,
Who knew a blanket could be so free?

Memories Woven in Dusty Corners

Forgotten boxes where treasures take breath,
Dust motes pirouette like dancers of death.
A frame that holds more than just a face,
Its eyes still twinkling, full of grace.

A shoehorn sings of a cobbler's delight,
While the old rug dreams of flights in the night.
Ticklish laughter interrupts the pause,
In corners where silence begins to thaw.

Echoes of Forgotten Laughter

Once we climbed the tree so high,
Where our dreams could touch the sky.
But then we tripped and fell with glee,
Landscaping the yard, just you and me.

Old cereal boxes made great hats,
Dancing like the silliest cats.
We played pretend with wooden swords,
Dueling over imaginary hordes.

Remember the time that pie flew past?
A daring flight that couldn't last.
We laughed so hard, the neighbors peered,
Wondering what nonsense we had steered.

Now the tablecloth's a hiding spot,
Underneath, we plot a new thought.
Creating chaos in our prime,
The echoes of our past, quite sublime.

Whispering Shadows of Yesterday

There once was a cat with a regal pose,
Who thought he ruled from his little nose.
He sat on the throne—a laundry pile,
A king who'd nap for a long, long while.

We'd sneak in snacks and giggle loud,
While he'd survey us, proud and cowed.
Each pounce a drama, we'd barely breathe,
As shadows danced on the floor beneath.

Oh, the whispers of secret plans,
Trading woes for marshmallow bands.
With every giggle, we'd shrink and grow,
Chasing shadows of tales from long ago.

Each corner held a funny blunder,
As we ventured out, a duo of thunder.
In the silence, our laughter played,
Moments of joy that never frayed.

Remnants of a Time Once Lived

We'd pile our bikes in a daring heap,
Riding through trails, not losing sleep.
And then we'd tumble, giggling away,
While nature joined our lively fray.

A leap from the swing was a grand affair,
As flies we'd dodge through the warm-paced air.
Each scrape and bruise, a badge of fun,
Adventures shared, and never just one.

The jars of marbles, all colors bright,
Held contests in the fading light.
We'd stake our claims, oh, what a fight,
Till laughter rang out, everything felt right.

These remnants linger, like a sweet shroud,
In a box of treasures, forever proud.
Each silly moment stitched our tale,
With threads of joy that never pale.

Portraits Encased in Silence

A portrait hangs, a somber face,
Where once there danced a silly grace.
With hats askew and socks unmatched,
When every day was brightly hatched.

We'd paint our dreams in colors bold,
And laugh when things went uncontrolled.
In every corner, a story's found,
Of whispered giggles that still resound.

The tickling breeze, a playful tease,
Left memories that still aim to please.
We'd chase the shadows, make them race,
Finding laughter in every place.

Now time's a canvas, the past still smiles,
Encased in silence for a while.
Yet, in our hearts, joy's sun will shine,
With every quirk, old tales align.

The Archive of Unseen Tears

In cupboards high where dust collects,
Old photographs and silly flecks.
A sock without a mate, it beams,
Yet whispers softly, life's wild dreams.

A jar of giggles, a bottle of sighs,
Stretched out laziness beneath clouded skies.
Paintings frown, they have no clue,
This isn't serious, just a circus zoo.

Notes from lunch, they're crumpled tight,
Promises made under starlit night.
The ghosts of dates now slip and slide,
With forked tongues, they tease and bide.

Oh, laughter echoes through these halls,
Where sanity stumbles, and chaos sprawls.
Each tear a joke, each sigh a jest,
In this museum of life, we never rest.

Labyrinths of Longing and Light.

In corners bright, where shadows meet,
A pair of shoes, my big toe's defeat.
I wander lost, sing silly songs,
As daylight dances and night lasts long.

The fridge hums tales of takeout joy,
Half-eaten crusts from a pizza toy.
I chase lost dreams like runaway kites,
In this maze of fancy, the clock ignites.

The mirror laughs at my tangled hair,
Reflects the quirks I hardly care.
A joyride heart on a wobbly wheel,
In motion, mazes that don't conceal.

With every turn, a chuckle brews,
In corridors lined with old sock shoes.
Embracing echoes from silly days,
My heart finds home in a playful maze.

Echoes of Forgotten Lullabies

A moonlit dance on creaky floors,
Where tales are told behind closed doors.
Whispers tumble like clumsy hounds,
As bedtime stories spin and bounds.

Underneath the bed, a monster yawns,
Tangled sheets and sleepy dawns.
The lullabies have all forgotten,
Where have the giggles fled, begotten?

Puppets play on strings of dreams,
While shadow puppets cast funny schemes.
I glimpse a world of mirth and ease,
In this kingdom, I'm the jester, please.

Old toys laugh at their rusty fate,
A teddy bear serves as my best mate.
With echoes ringing from the night,
We snicker softly until first light.

Shadows of Yesterday's Whispers

Once where silence tiptoed proud,
A playful heart now dances loud.
Socks on ceilings, oh what fun,
In this realm, we've just begun!

Chasing echoes of wild laughter,
Ghosts parade with silly chatter.
Each corner hides a truth absurd,
In shadows soft, the charm is stirred.

Forgotten cupcakes sprout from place,
With frosting magical, a sugared grace.
The past recites its sweetest tales,
As laughter rides on wobbly sails.

In this garden of past delights,
We plant our jokes on paper kites.
With every whisper, a ticklish breeze,
In shadows bright, we dance with ease.

Chasing Faded Footprints

Running after shadows, my feet feel light,
Stumbling on laughter that dances in flight.
Each corner I turn, a joke waits to bloom,
Reminders of antics that filled every room.

The old chair creaks in a sly, knowing tone,
It whispers of mischief when no one was home.
Dust bunnies giggle, they know all the schemes,
Of childhood adventures and wild, silly dreams.

A squeaky floorboard, a ghost of a laugh,
Takes me back swiftly, like a kid on a half.
I trip over memories, tangled and spry,
Each wall has a story, a wink from the sky.

Through corridors echoing giggles and sighs,
A treasure of nonsense in mischief-filled skies.
Chasing those footprints in dreams that we shed,
I find joy in the laughter, the echoes of red.

The Well of Silent Secrets

Peek into the depths where the whispers collide,
Secrets of pranks that were well kept inside.
A chuckle, a glimpse of a time warp machine,
Winks at the chaos that once intervened.

Water under bridges, or was it the floor?
Each drop tells a story of who came before.
Tiny fish swim in the sea of old jokes,
Fins flipping and flopping, as laughter provokes.

In the well's dark embrace, memories flicker,
A nod from the past that gets only slicker.
I toss in a penny, what wish should I claim?
Maybe a dance with the clowns that I blame.

The silence is heavy, yet giggles emerge,
From shadows that linger, a comical surge.
Down by the well, all the secrets unroll,
Old stories of jesters that once stole the show.

The Architecture of Reminiscence

Tall towers of fabric, stitched tight with old yarn,
Crafted with laughter, where mischief would spawn.
Brick by brick built on the puns of the past,
A structure of smiles, forever to last.

Windows wide open, with curtains that sway,
Each breeze brings a chuckle from yesterday's play.
The roof is a stage where performers would cheer,
Building castles of jokes, where no one sheds a tear.

Chimneys puff out old tales wrapped in glee,
Tickling the skies with their vibrant decree.
The framework of joy, strong yet so light,
In a house full of whimsy, where everything's bright.

With a door that squeaks messages to unfold,
It creaks in delight at the stories retold.
A blueprint of laughter, each room is a dream,
Turning memories mundane to a comical theme.

Voices Lost in Time

Echoes of laughter from corners unseen,
Whispers of antics that once were routine.
The tickle of time wears a funny disguise,
Leading the lost through a comedy's rise.

From deep in the attic, a chuckle heaves low,
Dust motes dancing as if putting on a show.
Voices spin tales about soup on the floor,
Every blush of the past opens up a new door.

The clock laughs aloud, as it stubbornly winks,
Ticking away, like it too needs some drinks.
Requests for a concert from clowns in the hall,
Take center stage, laughing as shadows befall.

In echoes, we find all the spirit divine,
Lost tales come alive, in the rhythm of time.
Voices still giggle, though faded and shy,
Reminding us all why we laugh till we cry.

The Mansion of Half-Remembered Dreams

In a grand house filled with squeaks,
Ghosts of my youth play hide and seek.
I trip on my own persistent haze,
And laugh at my life's forgotten ways.

Each corner has secrets and snacks,
Where I once thought I'd make great tracks.
But pillows hold tales I can't retrieve,
As mock memories cause me to grieve.

The portraits frown at my clumsy grace,
While dust bunnies dance in a silly space.
Their jokes are lost, but I still grin,
In this mansion where odd thoughts begin.

So toast to the quirks of a fading mind,
With half-eaten pies that time left behind.
I'll chuckle and dine on my dreams gone by,
In this whimsical home where we all say hi.

Footsteps Beneath the Dust

Each step echoes of laughter long past,
With shadows that wiggle and giggle so fast.
I wander through hallways of whacky old sights,
Where echoes once played in dazzling lights.

Dust piles gather, companions to roam,
They'd chat about days I'd forgot to comb.
With every squeak of the crooked floors,
I find new adventures behind old doors.

Forgotten records play tunes out of tune,
As I twirl with the memories beneath the moon.
The floorboards creak a familiar jest,
In this quirky place I love the best.

Before I trip on a ghost from my youth,
I'll laugh with the footprints and chase the truth.
For every stumble is a dance in disguise,
In this dusty realm where the past never lies.

Fragments of a Faded Past

Fragmented whispers of days gone wide,
Popcorn clouds and toys that want to hide.
I search for the crayons, they've all flown away,
In a time machine that steals my gray.

The swings in the yard creak softly with cheer,
As squirrels gossip secrets I barely hear.
Fragments of laughter bounce off the trees,
Reminding me of wild moments that tease.

With a wiggle and jiggle, I probe in the mist,
For treasures buried in my memory's list.
But they just giggle and run out of sight,
As I chase after echoes till day turns to night.

Oh, what a delight to spin in this dance,
With fragments of yesterdays urging my chance.
I embrace the odd bits that shimmer and gleam,
In this playground of life where I always dream.

The Heart's Archive of Moments

In a vault filled with giggles and grins,
I find the mistakes that made me win.
Each folder's stuffed with hilarious flops,
Memories tumble like colourful hops.

I sift through the laughs and cringe-worthy shows,
The tangled tales only my heart knows.
A scroll of mishaps that spark joy anew,
In the archives where love always flies true.

Scraps of romance and blunders galore,
Blend together to make my heart soar.
There's a dress that was once the highlight of fate,
But wore off its charm while I danced with fate.

So here in my archive, I chuckle and purr,
Each moment outshines the next little blur.
With merry missteps, I tiptoe and sway,
In the heart's great warehouse where smiles always play.

The Gallery of Lost Lullabies

Whispers hang on painted walls,
Dreams that once enthralled.
A tune that tickled every night,
Now just a ghost in flight.

Crib sheets dance with dust and cheer,
A comedy of yesteryear.
Songs that make you crack a smile,
Echo through this playful aisle.

Hushed giggles swirl in the air,
As if they're still unaware.
A lullaby that can't be found,
Just laughter lost without a sound.

Frames adorned with silly pics,
Arms raised in joyous tricks.
These tunes of joy, though long forgotten,
Are still alive, just slightly rotten.

Footprints on Dusty Floors

Tiny trails of laughter run,
Proof of mischief, just for fun.
Each footstep stamps a quirky tale,
A dance upon a winding trail.

Socks that slipped and shoes that squeaked,
Chasing giggles, moments peaked.
A floor that knows each tiny prank,
Like skids and slides down the plank.

Dust bunnies scatter at each step,
While ghosts of playtime deftly crept.
Fleeting footprints, quite absurd,
Telling stories without a word.

Each mark a giggle, every stain,
A memory wrapped in joy and pain.
Let's celebrate the chaos here,
With every laugh, we hold so dear.

The Resonance of Silent Corners

Corners hold the best of woes,
Where secrets peek and mischief grows.
A chair sits still, a witness keen,
To countless plots by kids unseen.

Dust collects in playful bands,
Where plans were hatched by tiny hands.
Voices linger, overlapping cheer,
In hushed recesses, deep and clear.

The echo of a giggle bright,
Bouncing gently through the night.
Each silence seems to hold a jest,
While shadows dance and laugh at rest.

In forgotten nooks, the joys reside,
With whispers that the walls confide.
These silent corners, oh so spry,
Crack silly jokes as time drifts by.

Secrets Beneath the Floorboards

Beneath the planks, the tales unwind,
Of sneaky plots, quirky and blind.
Dusty vaults of youthful schemes,
Where laughter lingers, or so it seems.

Marbles rolled with a clattering sound,
Echoing as they bounced around.
Lost treasures hide in splintered seams,
Whispers of immature dreams.

A stash of toys, oops, 'neath the bed,
With dust bunnies that have long fled.
Each secret, a giggle in disguise,
Waiting for fun to arise.

If only the floor could share its glee,
Of shadows dancing, wild and free.
Each creak and groan, a comic jest,
Beneath our feet, the past is blessed.

Embers of the Unremembered

Forgotten socks in a drawer
Dance like embers, evermore.
Lost keys play hide-and-seek,
Even the fridge has secrets to speak.

Crumbs hide under the couch,
Chasing off the curious pouch.
Remote controls have a life,
Like a sitcom filled with strife.

The cat stares at the wall,
Wondering if ghosts have a ball.
Dust bunnies planning their heist,
Hold a party, oh what a feast!

Pictures fade in the hall,
But stories linger, big and small.
A thick fog of laughs ensues,
Memories wrapped in silly hues.

Reveries Trapped in the Attic

In the attic, a hat takes flight,
Dusty tales of a chicken's fight.
Old toys giggle in the gloom,
As the spider spins a room.

Grandpa's trousers, two sizes too wide,
Mismatched socks take a joyful ride.
Squeaky shoes with stories to tell,
Dance around, under a spell.

A box of letters, yellowed and torn,
Hiding secrets from dreams unborn.
The clock ticks, but what can it say?
Time's just another game we play.

Amidst the cobwebs, laughter rings,
Echoes of past, and all that it brings.
A treasure trove of silly sights,
Reveries trapped in cozy nights.

A Symphony of Silent Echoes

The fridge hums a secret song,
About leftovers that have gone wrong.
A chair scoffs, creaks with glee,
At the meals that nobody can see.

Silhouettes dance on the wall,
As socks get lost in a whimsical brawl.
The curtains sway, a curtain call,
For the can of beans that stood too tall.

A sock puppet gives a wink,
Sharing whispers about the kitchen sink.
Echoes of laughter float and sway,
In the grand flurry of yesterday.

Oh, the tales that silence tells,
Through the walls, like ringing bells.
A symphony of oddities bright,
Colorful memories in plain sight.

Pictures Framed in Silence

On the wall, portraits grin wide,
With goofy faces that can't hide.
A dog wearing glasses, with flair,
Makes us wonder who's really there.

In a frame, a cat with a hat,
Planning schemes while it naps flat.
Photos hiding, cheeky and quaint,
A family reunion, filled with paint.

Empty frames hold stories untold,
About a wand that turned to gold.
The whispers echo through time's dance,
Inviting us all to join the chance.

Memories linger, sweet yet absurd,
In every glance and every word.
Pictures talk in a hushed delight,
Framed in silence, glowing bright.

Hidden Echoes of Laughter

Old socks dance in the dryer,
Singing songs of wild desire.
Dust bunnies hold a grand parade,
While the spoons plot their next charade.

Fridges hum a sleepy tune,
While leftovers scheme beneath the moon.
Each tick of the clock, a silent joke,
As the tea kettle dreams of a smoke.

Windows sigh with stories to tell,
As curtains whisper of their spell.
The cat naps on a pile of dreams,
Chasing fish in the sunlight beams.

Every creak is a laugh out loud,
While shadows play beneath the shroud.
In the nooks, mischief resides,
With giggles echoing where it hides.

A Mosaic of Forgotten Places

Postcards stacked beneath the bed,
Adventures lost, but laughter spread.
Coffee cups brim with old tales,
As the sugar stirs up whimsical gales.

Under the couch, an old shoe waits,
With secrets shared by playful mates.
The lamp jokes with the crooked hat,
As the rug rolls its eyes at the spat.

Walls blush with memories dim,
While chairs spin tales just on a whim.
The dust settles, a cozy shroud,
Beneath the laughter, hidden and loud.

A tapestry woven of chuckles and cheer,
In the corners, mischief lingers here.
Each room's a stage, where jesters prance,
In the gallery of fate, they twirl and dance.

The Diary of Broken Echoes

A diary sits with pages worn,
Filled with giggles and pranks, well-torn.
Ink spills tales of mischief's reign,
Of banana peels and lemonade rain.

Scribbles of joy in a crooked line,
Captured moments, both silly and fine.
Each doodle a laugh, every tear a song,
In the margins, where the winks belong.

Erasers dance, and pencils whirl,
As lunch boxes join in a swirl.
Forgotten notes of laughter play,
In a symphony of fun, come what may.

The diary sighs with a hearty chuckle,
As sticky notes gather for a cuddle.
In its pages, the echoes remain,
A monument built of joy and pain.

Chasing the Shadows of Time

Tick-tock goes the clock on the wall,
As shadows gather for their call.
They play hopscotch in dimming light,
Chasing slips of giggles through the night.

With each tick, a mischief unfolds,
Stories of silly times retold.
The grandfather clock holds its breath,
As the echoes tease the edges of death.

Rug rats tumble in mirrored spree,
While hats on hooks join in glee.
The past prances with a wink so sly,
As laughter weaves through moments, oh my!

Each shadow a jest, a prank in disguise,
Carving smiles as daylight dies.
We gather around for one last cheer,
As the echoes of joy draw near.

Secrets Etched in Ancestral Walls

Grandma swears she once had a cat,
Who danced on the table, just like that.
Her stories twist, they spin and sway,
I think it's the pickle jar's fault, I say.

A cousin once slipped and fell in stew,
Claimed high art was what he'd pursue.
But every family has tales that collide,
And the walls have seen more than our pride.

An uncle lost socks in the garden maze,
Thought he'd discover a treasure that pays.
But just found a shovel, a rusty old bike,
And laughed at the chaos, 'Well, what do you like?'

Memories smirk from each weathered nook,
Each creak and each groan holds a storybook.
In laughter and love, the past remains bold,
With humor unraveled, our secrets unfold.

Time's Gentle Embrace

Tick-tock goes the old grandfather clock,
It tells more tales than mere time on the block.
Like socks that are missing since '92,
Or dreams that were dared, but then never flew.

With each passing year, we laugh and we cheer,
Sharing old pranks that bring us near.
With each cup of tea, more giggles arise,
As we reminisce over baked apple pies.

Uncle Joe's mustache still steals the show,
It has lived more adventures than we could know.
With a swirl and a twirl, it tweaks tales anew,
And the walls listen closely, they giggle too.

The gentle embrace of laughter's delight,
Wraps us in warmth on a chilly night.
So let's toast to the years that keep rolling along,
In this crazy, wild life, we'll always belong.

Lanterns of the Heart's Recollection

Remember the night the cake flew awry?
With icing that soared as we all let out a sigh.
Laughter exploded like stars in the sky,
As Grandma retrieved her old secret supply.

There's the lantern that flickers with tales of glee,
Each flick for a thumb, each grin set free.
Like Dad's mischief, mending a lawnmower's grind,
That ended up with the neighbor, who was blind.

We spin our yarns, woven with light,
Of siblings who fought in a great made-up fight.
With lanterns aglow, we dance and we play,
As the shadows remind us of bright yesterday.

The outlines of laughter, a shimmering spark,
Illuminate corners that once were quite dark.
So here's to the lanterns that kindle our dreams,
In the warmth of laughter, nothing's as it seems.

Inscriptions of a Life Well-Lived

Carved in the cabinets, lies a cheap spoon,
A prize from a picnic in the heat of June.
The inscription reads 'Best Eater' with pride,
A title I earned with each mouth as my guide.

The couch has a dip where dear Uncle Lou,
Napped through the tales that he barely knew.
His dreams danced in rhythms, like socks on the floor,
As his snoring kept time with the family lore.

With each crack in the wall, a giggle's alive,
Of cousins who wrought mischief, oh how we thrive!
We etched all our moments in laughter and play,
Inscriptions of joy that will never decay.

So here's to the stories in cracks and in stains,
Of wild, wonderful lives served without any chains.
May we sip from this cup of nostalgia and cheer,
And treasure the antics that bring us all near.

Collapsed Stories of the Heart

A cat named Whiskers stole my shoe,
He stares like it's his rightful due.
I once had plans for her and me,
But shoe theft made her run for tea.

I laughed so hard, I spilled my drink,
I thought I'd drown in puppy stink.
Each sock a tale of how we bled,
And Whiskers plotting dreams instead.

The kind of love that makes you yawn,
With memories of a garden lawn.
Where daisies danced in silly hats,
And time sat still with silly cats.

Yet through the giggles, tears do flow,
As stories twist, then quickly go.
But I'll keep all the jumbled threads,
In fabric soft, where laughter spreads.

Time's Fleeting Portraits

Snapshots hang, all crooked smiles,
With every laugh, we went for miles.
A poodle danced on Grandma's lap,
While Cousin Timmy took a nap.

Mom's a chef with her burnt soufflé,
A masterpiece in disarray.
The picture frame, a bit askew,
But it captures joy in every hue.

Uncle Joe with his silly hats,
Jumping jacks and chatty chats.
Even when the time was thin,
We danced as if we'd always win.

Each portrait tells a tale so grand,
Of moments shared and silly band.
And in each laughter, brightly caught,
Are reminders of the joy we sought.

Memories Behind Stained Glass

A window cracked, with colors bold,
Stories of laughter, tales retold.
One time I slipped on Dad's old shoe,
And the glass exploded, right in two.

The sunlight beams through every crack,
Where echoes of a joke come back.
A parrot squawked a scene so raw,
As Mom just rolled her eyes in awe.

The family feast with pies galore,
A missed catch led to food war.
With whipped cream stuck in Uncle's hair,
A masterpiece beyond compare.

Yet through the glass, I see it clear,
Each giggle shared, each silly cheer.
A prism of our wacky past,
Reminds me how the fun can last.

The Weight of Unspoken Words

Between the lines, we hide our glee,
With awkward hugs and spilled sweet tea.
Like when I told my crush, 'You're great!'
But tripped instead, and sealed my fate.

We danced around what should be said,
Like handstands on a loopy bed.
Each silence weighed like heavy fluff,
Yet somehow, it was still enough.

The things we never dare to say,
Become the punchlines in the play.
And laughter echoes through the night,
As memories seem to take their flight.

In all the weight we choose to hold,
Lie funny tales of hearts so bold.
For every word we leave unsaid,
Turns into joy when laughter's spread.

Reflections on the Edge of Silence

When the cat jumped high with flair,
I swear, it looked like it had a scare.
It landed right on Grandma's hat,
And now it's her new funky cat!

A goldfish danced in its glass dome,
Thinking it had a real cool home.
But with every swish of its tail,
It missed the dog who snored and wailed.

In corners, whispers made us chuckle,
As Mom tried to shoo the dust with a buckle.
Each thud of the broom brought us glee,
More than the show on TV!

And who can forget Dad's old sock,
Stuck in the gears of the old clock?
Time stopped as we held our breath,
Laughter echoed, a sign of life and zest!

The Veil of Hidden Thoughts

A note was tucked inside a shoe,
'Wear the left one, it fits you!'
Mom found it, her face turned red,
Declaring, 'Now who wrote this, instead?'

Grandpa's stories made us yawn,
About his youth, dodging prawn.
But when he slipped on a banana peel,
Even he laughed, that was the deal!

The garden gnome gave a wink,
As Auntie played with the kitchen sink.
Her spatula flew up like a bird,
But nobody noticed, how absurd!

Beneath the stairs, a treasure lies,
Old board games and puppet spies.
We'd play till lights dimmed out,
Dinner forgotten, we'd laugh and shout!

Threads Woven in the Quiet

A pair of socks, mismatched and bright,
Were once a prize in a socks-off fight.
Mom rolled her eyes, but we knew the truth,
They hid a tale of wild, silly youth.

The chair squeaked a secret in the night,
As we snuck cookies, feeling just right.
With crumbs on our shirts, we'd laugh so free,
Knowing the roast was still in the sea!

An old guitar in the corner moaned,
Its strings whispered secrets long postponed.
But when we strummed, it tried to dance,
And gave us all a silly chance!

Every shadow seemed to have a grin,
As we played games, letting mischief in.
In whispers and giggles, we found our bliss,
Mom's raised eyebrow told us, "Now, calm this!"

Portraits in the Attic

Old pictures in frames that look so sly,
   Caught Uncle Joe with a pie, oh my!
With cream on his nose and a grin so wide,
   He pranced like a goat, taken in stride.

The attic creaked, full of dusty fun,
As we searched for treasures under the sun.
I'd found a cape, ruled like a king,
   Complete with a crown made from string!

Ghosts of teddy bears held a tea,
While monsters were munching on our glee.
Each laugh echoed, bouncing off the wall,
Who knew monsters made the best of a ball?

So here's to the laughter stored up high,
In corners where shadows can never die.
Each portrait, a giggle forever gold,
   Handed down stories fondly retold!

Portraits of What Might Have Been

Old photos laugh at me, so bold,
Dressed in styles that never get old.
Mustache twirling, hair so high,
I wonder why I said goodbye.

A dance-off with socked feet, oh dear,
Each twist and turn brings back a cheer.
Potato chips on the rug, a feast,
I swear, my youth was quite the beast!

Bubblegum pop and carefree days,
Why did we think we'd earn our praise?
Now I'm here with this crazy crew,
Pretending our dreams could come true.

With every chuckle, a truth revealed,
Life's absurdity is truly sealed.
In the gallery of my heart,
These goofy moments won't depart.

An Odyssey of Fleeting Moments

Once I swam in a cereal pool,
Fighting sharks with a spatula tool.
My cape was a towel, I was so grand,
But today I just can't make a stand.

Mismatched socks on a pizza spree,
Accidental mischief turns into glee.
Chasing echoes from halls of fun,
A game of tag that's never done.

Remember that time we built a fort?
With pillows stacked like a strange resort!
We served up soda, our finest meal,
There was laughter that time could not steal.

Though time has flitted, we hold it tight,
Those quirks of childhood bring pure delight.
So here we dance like it's still our day,
In our hearts, we forever play.

The Timelessness of Yesterday

When I ran in circles, pants down low,
Chasing dreams like they were all a show.
Sometimes I wonder, where did it go?
That silly bravado, the child in tow.

I wore my brother's shoes, what a sight,
He tackled me down in the late moonlight.
Laughter echoed, and I lost my shoe,
Now with old sneakers, how time flew.

At lunchtime sneaking snacks from his stash,
With crumbs left behind, oh what a clash!
We schemed and plotted, our secret plot,
That endless mischief hits the right spot.

The magic of ages hangs in the air,
We grasp at the giggles, a vibrant flare.
So hold those memories, though times may bend,
Today's silliness is never the end.

Delicate Threads of Nostalgia

In the attic, dust bunnies roam free,
Toys and trinkets are laughing at me.
Silly hats outshine the fashion,
A parade of giggles is in full action.

I found a diary with dreams to bake,
Muffins of joy, what a glorious mistake!
Each page a snapshot of days gone past,
With doodles of dragons, memories vast.

Kites that tangled up in trees so high,
Whispers of secrets just you and I.
In the fabric of laughter, we stitched a thread,
Of colorful moments that never quite fled.

So here's to the quirks, the love, the jest,
Time's funny family, we're truly blessed.
With every chuckle, a smile arrives,
In the threads of nostalgia, our spirit thrives.

The Archive Beneath the Skin

Inside my head, there's quite a mess,
Where lost socks hold their own success.
A circus of thoughts, doing cartwheels,
Juggling old laughs, that's how it feels.

Each wrinkle's a ticket to a show,
Where lawn chairs and dreams sit all aglow.
I swear I had a plan, once upon a time,
But it fled on a bus, without reason or rhyme.

Memories giggle, they dance and they play,
An orchestra of mishaps on display.
I throw confetti at past regrets,
And marvel at chaos—my bestest pets!

So here's to the madness that keeps me awake,
A scrapbook of moments, some real, some fake.
With each silly thought, I silently grin,
For the joy is alive, buried deep within.

Fragments of a Faded Mind

A pot of soup with too many cooks,
In a kitchen of memories, there are strange books.
Like jigsaw puzzles with missing parts,
Comedic escapes from the mundane arts.

Old photographs, all crooked and worn,
Tell stories of mishaps the kids had sworn.
Wobbly chairs and spilled lemonade,
Each sip was a laugh, a moment well-made.

The clock says it's time for my daily nap,
But the cat on my lap has set a new trap.
As dreams play hide-and-seek on my mind,
I chase after laughter that's one of a kind.

Each fragment I find, I read it and ply,
Silly anecdotes swirling up to the sky.
I'll chuckle at wrinkles and giggle at time,
For life is a joke, and I'm in my prime!

Secrets in the Cracks

Beneath the floorboards, a treasure waits,
Dust bunnies hosting some wild debates.
They compare old fables and silly things,
While the clock in the corner secretly sings.

Cracks in the walls whisper jokes I forgot,
About the time I played hopscotch on the spot.
The echoes of laughter escape like a ghost,
As I stumble on tales of what matters most.

Under the cushions, lost toys still scheme,
Holding meetings on how to live the dream.
They giggle at memories, loud as a cheer,
While I trip on the past, still drawing me near.

With every creak, there's a ticklish tease,
The house holds my secrets with effortless ease.
So here's to the laughter, both near and far,
In the corners of rooms where the wild things are!

Time's Silent Palimpsest

Time writes its stories on parchment and air,
In invisible ink, it does not seem fair.
But old notes and doodles come back from the past,
Like pigeons with tales of their journeys vast.

On scraps of paper, I find bits of fun,
A doodle of cats and a half-eaten bun.
Each smudge is a trace of a laugh lost to age,
As I sift through the pages, I take center stage.

A comical timeline, so convoluted,
With pratfalls and blunders, perfectly suited.
Like a pair of mismatched socks on parade,
Every stitch tells a tale, no plans need be made.

As time flips the pages, the stories unfold,
Bringing warmth to the heart, making memories bold.
So I cherish the laughter from moments gone by,
In the ledger of life, oh me, oh my!

The Silent Witnesses of Time

Old chairs creak tales in the night,
Pants from the past, oh what a sight!
Dust bunnies dance, oh so spry,
While memories giggle and sigh.

The clock ticks loud, like a drum,
It hears the whispers of what we become.
Jars of buttons, odd and round,
Gerbil like moments, spinning around.

Pictures smirk from walls so bold,
Faded jokes that never get old.
Timeless laughter in silent halls,
Echoes of clumsy, fun-filled falls.

Now we sit, sipping our tea,
With the silent witnesses, just you and me.
Time may age, but oh what a jest,
Even in silence, we're truly blessed.

Bottled Memories in the Attic

Up in the attic, treasures galore,
Bottled giggles behind that door.
A sock puppet's laugh, oh what a tease,
While spiders weave webs with perfect ease.

A hat from a party, feathers askew,
It tells of nights when silly was new.
Labeled jars, full of glittering mists,
Each one a giggle that simply insists.

Old letters crinkle, penned with delight,
Where secrets and rhymes sparked joy in the night.
A fizzy soda named "Yesteryear",
With every sip, we felt no fear.

Close the lid softly, don't let it fade,
These bottled sprinkles in time are made.
Lift your glass to the magic we find,
In the attic, laughter is unconfined.

Reflections on an Old Mirror

A mirror whispers, 'Aren't you bright?'
With a smirk, it shares tales of delight.
Cracked corners hint at outlandish style,
It reflects a grin, that's quite worth the while.

Each smudge holds a secret, what a show,
From lopsided hair to a misplaced bow.
It remembers the dances, awkward yet bold,
The promise of youth — ah, manifold.

In the frame, laughter and shadows entwine,
A duet of memories, perfectly fine.
Yesterday's wisdom, a show of rare cheer,
As we blunder with grace, the mirror draws near.

So here's to the glass that's seen it all,
With every reflection, we rise and we fall.
A wink from our past, oh what a sight,
In every giggle, the future feels bright.

The Chronicles of Fleeting Time

Once upon a tick, in a land so bright,
Chronicles scribbled by the firelight.
Where socks would disappear, and then reappear,
Crafting tales that just bring us cheer.

Pages turned with a crinkly sound,
Each one a moment, hilarity found.
Adventures of cats stuck up in trees,
Chasing after shadows, or bumblebee sneeze.

Fleeting seconds dance like fireflies,
Blink and they're gone, oh how time flies!
Yet laughter remains in the tales that we weave,
In the chronicles shared, we refuse to grieve.

So let's gather 'round, with smiles on our face,
As we flip through the chapters, at a giggly pace.
For time may be fleeting, but joy can be stout,
In these tales of ours, there's never a doubt!

The Labyrinth of Forgotten Faces

I stumbled on a face I swear,
It winked at me, I gasped in care.
A nose like bananas, much too round,
In memories lost, they still abound.

A grin from a chef now burns my bread,
In dreams, he tosses pie instead.
The neighbor's cat, a dapper chap,
Stole my socks for a glorious nap.

Old friends pop up, like popcorn's dance,
They spin and twirl in a silly trance.
With mismatched shoes, they try to impress,
Forgotten tales in quirky dress.

The maze of faces, a jester's ball,
Each corner turned, I laugh and stall.
With every laugh, a memory pours,
Bright confetti from memory's shores.

A Chronicle of Faded Pages

Once written down with a flourish bright,
Now I squint just to read the light.
A doodle there of a duck in a hat,
It quacks in my ear like an old-time brat.

The pages flip with a creak and sigh,
Telling tales of when I could fly.
A dance recital, or was it a meal?
I tripped on spaghetti, oh what a deal!

A recipe vague, notes lost in the flurry,
Was it sugar or salt? Oh, my head's in a hurry!
The stains on the edges, a snack attack,
Each bite taken, a laugh, a quack.

So I gather my crumbs, the stories anew,
Each page a snapshot, each memory's hue.
The laughter they hide, the secrets they weave,
I chuckle and grin, I will never leave!

Unraveling the Fabric of Time

Time's a fabric, with holes and threads,
I poke my finger, it laughs and spreads.
A sock from the past, it dances away,
I chase it down with a feathery sway.

A watch that ticked 'til it ran away,
"Time flies!" they say, but what do they pay?
I can't find my pants, lost in the chase,
Each ticking second, a comical race.

Forgotten birthdays come back with glee,
Like balloons that float, so carefree.
Each year's a party, the cake's always stale,
But the laughter rings out, we never fail.

So here's to the fabric that weaves us in fun,
In the patchwork of life, we dance and run.
With snags and frays, we twirl around,
The joy in our hearts is what we've found.

The Keeper of Hidden Truths

I guard the truths like candy so sweet,
Yet my memory's messy, a tangled feat.
A secret revealed, and oh what a laugh,
A squirrel in a tie with a funny staff.

Wandering through rooms, I stumble with cheer,
Each hidden truth's had a pint of beer.
The cat's on the floor, wrapped in old yarn,
Has it really been days, or is it just dawn?

In closets of nonsense, I giggle and peep,
Finding old toys that I meant to keep.
A rubber chicken and a dusty old shoe,
The relics of joy that once flew.

For laughter's the keeper of truths so divine,
Embracing the chaos, we sip on the vine.
With every giggle, a secret replays,
In the gallery of glee, I'll forever stay.

Beneath the Surface of Time

Beneath the surface, laughter hides,
Old socks and secrets, where time abides.
Tickling tales of oddity,
Sneaking past the privacy.

Riding on a whimsy breeze,
Faded memories tease with ease.
A banana peel or two,
And spills that never quite construe.

Faces from design old books,
Grinning back with playful looks.
Time, the jester of our days,
Winks and giggles in strange ways.

So here's to dancing years gone by,
Where moments trip and tumble shy.
In a field of forgotten sights,
Jokes linger on like fireflies.

Echoes of Solitude's Embrace

In echoes soft where silence plays,
My socks have formed conspiracy ways.
They hide beneath my chair with glee,
    Plotting how to embarrass me.

Once I spilled my dreams of cake,
Right into a pond for a fishy shake.
Yet solitude just laughed aloud,
    Making ripples, proud and loud.

A dog in a hat, so dapper, quite,
Chased his tail with all his might.
That's how memories softly dance,
    In pauses of a goofy prance.

So here's to the quirks, absurd and bright,
In the quiet, where's the overlap of light?
Let's gather the jests, both near and far,
    And toast to the quirks that we are!

The Quiet Murmurs of History

Whispers of the past, oh what a tease,
Painting pictures with clumsy ease.
An old potato, a smile stuck,
He reminisces of bad luck.

Knocking boots upon the floor,
Soundtrack of slaps we can't ignore.
History's hiccups, quite the show,
Strutting memories, here we go!

Butterflies dressed as lords of lore,
Flap about and settle on the floor.
They giggle at the tales we sweep,
In shadows where the past does creep.

Steamers of laughter float the air,
Where sandwiches danced without a care.
What a curious way to remember,
Through chuckles that light up the ember!

Cobwebs on Yesterday's Dreams

Cobwebs spun with dreams unsaid,
Tickle the thoughts that bounce in the head.
Strings of laughter held in place,
By the trusty whisper of space.

Old slippers lounge on yesterday's floor,
Teasing the echoes of what's in store.
Marshmallow clouds drift overhead,
Mapping out the paths we tread.

Nosey mice with top hats and flair,
Holding parties without a care.
Silly antics from dusk till dawn,
In the corners where dreams have gone.

So here's to cobwebs, a sticky delight,
Dusted off with quirky insight.
With every laugh, every sigh,
Yesterday's wonders are passing by.

www.ingramcontent.com/pod-product-compliance
Lightning Source LLC
Chambersburg PA
CBHW062112280426
43661CB00086B/551